CW00858805

ABOUT THE AUTHOR

Diana Chan is a passionate young entrepreneur. After graduating at University College London (UCL), she started 'Inspire Me Korea', her own company at the age of 21. She wishes to inspire and empower others who are equally determined, hard working and willing to take risks. She understands the difficulties for young adults aiming to carve their own path and hopes this book will guide those talented individuals who are considering entrepreneurship to lead and to share their visions.

INSPIRING
YOUNG ENTREPRENEURS

50 Things You Must Be Prepared For

DIANA CHAN
Founder and CEO at Inspire Me Korea

ISBN: 1530782724
ISBN-13: 978-1530782727

DEDICATION

For leaving me with the greatest gift, this is for my
late grandma,
the most supportive and loving mother,
my dearest sister, Alice,
those who have inspired and will inspire me,
and you who is in pursuit of your dreams.

INTRODUCTION

Thanks to everyone I've met on the road which has led me here, I can wake up and smile on a rainy day, go to bed every night being most grateful. If you want to learn a bit more about my background and how I became a CEO at the age of 21, you can find out at the end of this book, but most importantly, this book is about you. For having experienced the toughest moments in my life so far, but being able to enjoy the best feeling in the world - I want to share this with you.

If after reading this book, you are either burning to get cracking on your idea, or you've been entirely put off, congratulations.

I've always made a point that with entrepreneurship you should be all in or don't try at all. This is why a clear picture of what you're getting yourself into is imperative. There are equal bad parts to good when it comes to entrepreneurship and you need to be ready to tackle anything that you can foresee, as well as be prepared that you will be thrown off by the things that cannot be foreseen.

I came to write this book as I was inspired by one of my good friends, but also because I know clearly how difficult it can be when you're starting out. Being young is a huge advantage in terms of our mentality and drive, but also a disadvantage in terms of experience. I want to share the lessons I've learnt so far, and prepare you for the journey that you will be faced with. Often times, entrepreneurship can only be seen from third person, whilst the backend is an unspoken uphill battle. Before I started my company, I did not and could not imagine the range of obstacles and the infinite aspects to managing my own business. I imagined all of the perks and thought as long as I worked hard, I will achieve. Instead, entrepreneurship stands for uncertainty - uncertainty of whether you will make it, despite the investments of your time, effort and money.

As a young adult, you're only just finding your feet. As a young entrepreneur, you're going to stumble again and again along the way. Entrepreneurship is a battle, it is not a smooth journey, because no matter how much research you do and how many business plans you write, something will pop up unexpectedly. The reality is that making something out of nothing is difficult, it takes a strong personality to continuously persevere, work hard, endure numerous restless nights, burden the responsibility of your failures or successes and it is imperative to have the ability to tell yourself that there is nothing to fear, to keep going, continue to face challenges and embark on a new journey. 'Uncertainty' is the risk you are taking as an entrepreneur, but if your heart is in it, if you sincerely want to start your business, you can be powerful.

This book will inform, frighten, and simultaneously inspire. It aims to tell you the ups and downs of owning your own business, what you need to prepare, and reveal the truth about entrepreneurship. But most of all, tell you that it is all worth it - you will experience the most valuable life lessons and you will be so proud of yourself.

NB Some of the points are slightly exaggerated for humour purposes...

1 YOU ARE FORCED TO GROW UP

So far the toughest decisions you had to make was deciding what to eat for dinner.

Now a few months down the line, your toughest decision is who to hire and who to fire.

As the CEO, your emotions need to be cast aside so that the quality of your brand is not compromised. This is not easy to accomplish, especially when friends are involved. You have to make the best decisions for your company and this is why, the process of entrepreneurship will make you develop, grow and mature.

2 YOU ARE A THINKER AS MUCH AS A DO-ER

What sets you apart from your counterparts is that you are a go-getter. You're a change-maker.

You have a gnawing hunger to take on new tasks. You want to make things happen, so even when you said you'll take the weekend off, somehow you end up working on something related to your start-up.

Every day you want to advance that little bit more, to get closer to where you want to be (even if that means you become a workaholic).

Because you don't just dream. You get in that plane and drive yourself there.

3 THERE IS NO LINE BETWEEN WORK AND PRIVATE TIME

This is a huge issue for entrepreneurs.

There is no line between work and leisure, because our work is leisure, and leisure is work!

So it is not unusual to be in hibernation mode for a while. Becoming an anti-social being is not always an option we choose.

Having piles of work to do, from writing blog posts to tedious website designing and replying to copious number of emails, sometimes we just can't leave the house for a week or two.

Especially at the beginning stages of a start-up, it is exhilarating and you just can't stop working, so every day is work. Then, when you start to pick up speed and you can spare some time for other hobbies, you begin to receive several emails from people who are interested to collaborate or interview you. This leads to a snowball effect, you arrange meetings and spend your spare time preparing for them and congratulations, you are now working 24/7.

4 WHEN YOU GO SHOPPING WITH YOUR FRIENDS, THEY ARE LOOKING AT THE CLOTHES AND YOU ARE LOOKING AT THE BRAND

It's a day out with the friends post hibernation to stock up on the new trends of the season. They're picking up clothes from the rails and ready to try them on. On the other hand, you're unconsciously scrutinising the brands and their marketing strategy; from the logo design to the social media posts, the adverts, the colour scheme and how the brand incorporates subtle meaning to packaging.

Unfortunately, I don't think this can be undone.

5 SOME OF THOSE 'FRIENDS' WILL BECOME HATERS

Suddenly you will receive hundreds of friend requests and people who you haven't spoken to in years (perhaps those high school bullies) will start to seep back into your life again.

They will send you messages of congratulations and tell you how proud of you they are.

There will also be outright haters.

Then there will be good friends who become envious and spiteful.

There is a simple answer to avoid the haters. Do what is not worth talking about. Be average. Do nothing, and no one will notice you.

6 YOU WILL BE JUDGED

An abundance of standards are projected onto you as a young adult, that you almost feel suffocated and coerced into certain educational or career paths. Whether it is from your family or friends, when everyone is following the same path, you may concede out of fear and/or respect for those who are telling you what to do.

If you are sure of what you want to do, do it.

Those who are experienced, with no disrespect, do not see what you see. We are a different generation, and your idea is valuable. Not everyone can empathise and see from your perspective. They don't understand - they may not be your target market and they have never heard of your idea before. It doesn't mean it's not amazing.

It is great to receive advice from those who are experienced, but carefully weigh how valuable and how much you can transfer their advice to your market.

If you are willing to put in the work, no one has the right to stop you.

7 SUPPORT IS IMPORTANT

Support in any shape or form drives you to reach the next step and keep you looking ahead. From the smallest gesture - a 'follow' or a 'like' on a social page, a comment about your services or someone saying that they've heard of your brand when you meet them for the first time is of phenomenal importance and something you will never forget. All of these gestures are priceless.

You are not alone in wanting to create this vision and other people are starting to notice your hard work.

Simultaneously, there will be at least one person who is constantly channelling negativity to you. They keep putting you down, telling you that what you're doing is not valuable, it's a waste of time, you've not got the right attitude. They will keep putting you down - until you get rid of them. There is often a clear difference between constructive criticism, envious comments and genuinely negative people. If they're envious and negative, make sure you cut them out fast. You don't have time or energy to waste.

Focus. The last thing you want is to be distracted and dragged down.

Don't let any of the negativity sway you.

8 YOU HAVE TO MAKE SELFISH DECISIONS

You want to hang out with your friends just a little longer.

One more hour?

No, tomorrow is Sunday and your friends can have a lie in, but you need to be awake and working at 5am to finish a blog post which should be up by 9am on Sunday, so everyone who has a day off will have time to read the post.

So, now you're known as 'the party pooper' because you have to go home.

Entrepreneurs have to make sacrifices, at least at the beginning stages of the venture, where you have piles of work waiting for you and you have to organise your priorities.

9 YOU NEVER HAVE A SET SCHEDULE

You'll have friends that constantly ask to meet up, followed by 'what days are you free?' to which you have no answer. Every day is different.

Instead, you answer 'What days are you usually free? I'll contact you on one of those days…'

10 YOU ARE IN YOUR OWN WORLD

At first, you may feel like you're missing out on life. People ask you 'Have you seen _____ (insert famous film name here)' and you say 'what's that?'

At this point you only know about formulas in spreadsheets, who your competitors are and where's the best place to buy your takeaway.

You'll be in your own world for a while, but enjoy it. This is when you're most focused and anything outside of your bubble could distract you - hey, building your dream takes sacrifices.

Prepare yourself, you won't be going to get a haircut or going to the gym, let alone cinemas and anything fancy for a good while.

Enjoy the hustle.

11 YOU WANT TO SHRIVEL UP AND DISAPPEAR WHEN SOMEONE MENTIONS 'FINANCIAL PLAN'

Can I just skip it?

Those two words are traumatising.

12 YOU BECOME CONFIDENT IN PITCHING YOUR BUSINESS IDEA

At the beginning, you're terrified.

You don't want to see the audiences' reactions, because you don't want to be faced with a majority of puzzled faces, or worse, displeased.

You're afraid to talk about it, even in the most relaxed situations. You find the briefest way to mention your idea in everyday conversation and then move on swiftly.

Now, you've been through it enough times, and you no longer care.

You know very clearly that your idea is awesome, and those who don't acknowledge it do not matter. You start to enjoy doing elevator pitches and going into detail about your idea, because you are confident. You know what you're doing.

13 YOU HOLD DEEP CONVERSATIONS WITH FELLOW ENTREPRENEURS

You attract entrepreneurs like a magnet, and once you get talking about the best and worst of entrepreneurship you can talk for weeks.

There are many people I've met throughout this short journey so far who have built their own brands, started a business or want to start a business and have approached me to discuss the struggles associated. It is always very inspiring and meaningful to meet like-minded people and to share common problems. We feed off of each other's enthusiasm and introduce people who may be of great value to the other party.

Entrepreneurship is not lonely at all after the initial stage, if anything, we create a community of people who support each other and are there to give advice or share their experiences, because we know how hard it is to work on something on your own.

Even if the industries are worlds apart, you have so many things in common.

14 NO MATTER HOW CONFIDENT YOU ARE, YOU WILL DOUBT YOURSELF

Despite how confident you are, there will be a small niggling worry inside you. When you put some thought into it, you will realise that you're petrified. You're petrified that at some point you might make the wrong move and the castle you've been building will fall to ruins, or worse, an enemy, an invader will knock it all down.

The first 6 months prior to launching my start-up, every day I woke up feeling excited to fulfil the tasks which will bring that 'to be completed' bar up to 100%. Every day it was a struggle to complete the endless task list, but I was eager to tick them off. At the same time, there is this strange intense feeling of excitement mixed with worry. There would be a small piece of me that was petrified. Petrified that my vision would fail in the transition to becoming a product.

Entrepreneurship is based on uncertainty. The burden of uncertainty is the price for not doing what everyone else is. Full time jobs at a reputable company are secure, they promise you certain perks and of course, a salary that will always be in your account at the end of the month. Entrepreneurship is about risking all of that.

You ask yourself 'are you sure this will work?' 'What if it doesn't?' Being a sole founder is especially hard, you're making decisions alone and you find yourself questioning your own abilities. You have no one to fall back on. No one to tell you - I believe it will work, let's keep going. Well, I will tell you that. There are people out there waiting for you to appear, waiting to embrace you and tell you 'I've been waiting for you'. Don't overthink, just do.

15 MAKE MISTAKES WHILE YOU'RE YOUNG

When you were young, do you remember what you said you wanted to be when you grew up? Do you remember how brave you were to learn something new?

As adults, we overthink, we become more fearful and afraid of losing something, failing and making mistakes. We become embarrassed by our mistakes. We stop doing new things, imagining, creating, we stop listening to our instincts. We stick to what we know, because that is what we are most confident in. When we are confident, we feel comfortable.

You can afford to make mistakes. You can afford to fail. You're young and you have nothing to lose. If anything, you have everything to learn.

When you meet someone who is very skilled at something which you wish you were also skilled at, and you think, 'if only I started learning that a couple of years ago, I would be great at it now'. Well, start now. Your future self will thank you.

It's never too late to start something new.

16 YOUR ENTHUSIASM WILL INSPIRE OTHERS

Enthusiasm is contagious.

Your love for what you are creating and providing for your customers, your care for their problem that you are aiming to solve shows them that you are not just bringing a product to the market and receiving profit. You are deeply concerned about whether your customers like the product, whether it solves their problem, whether the user experience can be improved.

My company stands for something I am strongly passionate about. Every time I am asked to explain about my company, I'm eager to talk about it. I am keen to tell the story of how I came to create this brand and share my passion with anyone who is equally excited about it. All the time, I can feel the listener is highly engaged, they tell me that they can feel my passion and my drive to share this passion.

Because of this, I have met new people who share the same intense dedication to what I care about, and we become great friends instantly. This includes customers.

This is utterly important in a start-up; your attitude towards your work and those who you wish to share your work with. You will unconsciously inspire others through your enthusiasm.

17 EVERY MINUTE COUNTS

Never have you ever fiercely raced against time until you have a start-up. Streamlining and cutting out anything that doesn't add enough value to your life becomes your first aim. You will eat meals on the way to meetings. Open the post on the tube, reply to emails while walking to the bus stop, make phone calls whilst you get ready in the morning. You start wondering what else you can cut out of your life to save another minute…

Don't worry.

There is a period where you're thrown into the deep end, and you just have to keep juggling those balls to keep things going. It's ok. At the next stage, things will be easier, it will be more organised, you will eventually create a routine that works for you, and this will give you some space to breathe.

Hustle hard and work smart, but don't overwork. Schedule your day and make to do lists to keep on track. Sometimes it will be more hectic than others, in which case, resting is not an option, just try not to neglect vital components that will keep you going in the long run.

18 YOU WILL BE ETERNALLY EXHAUSTED

Entrepreneurs don't run on sleep. They run on sheer perseverance, stubbornness and the will to prove people wrong. That's why you should do what you love. It will keep you wanting more, it will wake you up in the morning (or in the middle of the night), it will provide you with enough energy to last you days without sleep - because you want it desperately.

You can't stop working on your vision, not only because you can't wait to make it a reality, but also because you don't know how long you can last. Entrepreneurship is competitive. There are many eyes watching you and observing you. Got a good idea? Someone else has too. Just launched? Someone is replicating it. This is inevitable, and to keep guarding your precious ideas and hard work, you need to work even harder. Make yourself the best in the industry. Even then, you need to keep working to maintain that crown. Being the best is a burden, there's nowhere else to go but down. These thoughts will haunt you. You have to be able to accept these realities, be enthusiastic and ready to get your hands dirty.

Entrepreneurs are action-oriented bunch of people. Although it is overwhelming and pressurising, make sure you don't burn out. Frequent long hours can harm the body physically and mentally. Fatigue will indefinitely lead to plummeting productivity, and you don't want that. A break from chronic work will grant you a more innovative and creative mind.

Although on the bright side, it makes you so grateful to pack in a few hours of sleep here and there, you begin to appreciate all the small things and complain less!

19 WHEN SOMEONE ASKS YOU WHAT YOU DID ON THE WEEKEND…

You wish you had a better story to tell, but you replied to emails, snuggled on the sofa with an entrepreneur book and took a shift at your part time job on Saturday, and then spent Sunday making a GANTT chart (and you already know the schedule will not go as planned).

So instead, you just smile and reply 'it flew by! What did you do?'

20 YOU ARE JUGGLING A FEW PART TIME JOBS

What gets you through the day at your part time job is the cheque at the end of the day - not to spend on fancy clothes and shoes, but to pay for the bare necessities like rent, travel, and food. Part time jobs help to keep you safe from depleting to rock bottom.

It is funny how a lot of people have a misconception that young entrepreneurs must be rich. Maybe we will be soon, and we most definitely hope so. But many people assume that you come from a wealthy background to be able to support your big dreams.

This is by far the most incorrect assumption.

Of course there are some who are backed by a wealth of fortune to support businesses, but it is especially heartbreaking to see that this is often assumed to be the case when it is not.

This crushes young entrepreneurs because to fuel these big dreams of ours, we work even harder than everyone else, we juggle part time jobs and cut our spending to the point where we become desperate when Christmas comes along.

It's not easy to shrug off these assumptions and labels put on us, it is really unsettling to know that others are discrediting all the hard work you've put into your dream.

21 YOUR PART TIME JOB SUDDENLY FEELS LIKE REST DAY

When your 'day off work' is busier than your days at work, you will start to feel better about that part time job.

So if you're looking for a way to enjoy your part time job, just make your days off work restless.

22 YOU ARE OFFENDED WHEN SOMEONE SAYS 'YOU'RE SO LUCKY…'

Your start-up is the most precious thing to you.

You spend all your time protecting it and keeping it alive that you almost forget to keep yourself alive.

When someone says 'you're so lucky to have your own business', it is rather insulting. As much as it sounds like a compliment, our hard work is dismissed and instead, is accounted for as 'luck'; success brought by chance rather than purposeful action and tough grind.

Those who make such a remark are those who only see the end achievements, the photos of you throwing a party to celebrate the success of your company. They don't see the thousands of emails you sent, to which you only received one reply. They don't see the amount of times the answer was 'no', before you met the person that said 'yes'. For every plan that worked out, there were fifty others that were made. For every final product, there were hundreds that failed to make it to the market. For every step you took going forward, you stumbled and were pushed back, like walking against strong tides.

If we were to leave it to 'luck' to succeed, we will always be waiting.

23 YOU HAVE LOST TRACK OF WHAT DAY IT IS

You keep your head down. You live to accomplish the tasks of the day and know what your schedule is for the day after.

Suddenly you realise you're halfway into the new year already and the year is far from 'new' anymore.

24 YOU ARE LOST. YOU ARE SO LOST, BUT YOU ARE FINDING YOURSELF

You feel like you should know what you're doing at this point, you should be in control of your life, have everything planned out with clear goals for the coming years. Life just doesn't always work like that.

It baffles me when we are forced to make crucial life choices at such a young age. How can we make informed decisions?

Likewise, you have a vision, but you don't know where to start and where to go. Sometimes the furthest you can see is the next step ahead of you. When people ask you 'where do you see yourself in 5 years?' and you think 'why would you expect me to know that!?'

We're all lost at times but through realising what we want to do, every step of the way we are finding ourselves and realising our potential.

25 YOU WILL BE THE MOST DISORGANISED-ORGANISED PERSON

Let's face it. We all want to get our shit together, or at least look like we do. But of course, you're lost and confused.

It's like those bedrooms that are so messy, anyone who walks in will trip at least three times - over your clothes, leftover pizza from 2 nights ago and your bundle of charger cords, but, you still manage to find everything you need and know exactly where everything is.

Well, your life will also be the same.

You will have multiple meetings, places you need to go, phone calls to make, emails to reply, receipts scattered around - there's too much on your plate. Nonetheless, you will somehow work around it and the show goes on.

Sometimes, you will wish so hard that you could duplicate yourself.

26 YOU ARE RESPONSIBLE FOR EVERYTHING

You'll wear many hats, especially if you have little funds to hire someone to do a job for you. Starting my company on my own gave me so many opportunities to learn about an array of careers - I was the photographer, designer, blogger, magazine editor, web developer, accountant, marketing, customer service, brand ambassador…

The list goes on. You will enjoy some, you will hate some, and there will be something you will never understand! Whatever the case, there is just something magical when you can genuinely say "yes, I did it all". Building every aspect of a brand from scratch and proudly owning it, pretty much requires spending every waking hour pursuing the vision, but through this, you will be able to see the brand from different angles.

When filming promotional videos, I could experience the fun, three dimensional and liveliness of the brand. When developing the website design, it was about convenience and user experience, and researching website interfaces. When writing the magazines, it took hours to thumb through other magazines to capture the right tone of voice. Each aspect showed the same brand in a different light, and it forced me to work on the details and think deeply about what the brand stands for.

You will realise that there are a lot of things you had no idea you had to do, but now you have to. You will learn and grow from these experiences, love doing the things you already know and possibly learn about something new and realise you love it too! Whatever the case, when you're building something out of nothing, you have to do what you have to do, before you can do what you want to do.

27 YOU CANNOT DEPEND ON ANYONE

Other people have their commitments and priorities and chances are, your start-up is not one of them. By depending on others to deliver on time, or deliver at all, is a huge risk you're taking.

Very quickly you will realise that working on it yourself is a much safer and hassle-free option.

28 WHEN SOMEONE SAYS 'I HOPE YOU AND YOUR TEAM HAVE A GREAT DAY!'

You hide a little giggle because the team consists of a lonely me, a hungry me, and a sleep deprived me.

Thanks for appreciating my work and believing there's a herd of us bringing you all the content and replying to your emails at 2am.

29 SOMETIMES EVERYTHING FEELS LIKE IT IS FALLING APART

A lot of the time things fall apart before they can start to fall into place. At that moment, you need to stay strong.

It is hard to blindly believe, but don't lose faith. Whatever difficulties you're going through right now are temporary and they're supposed to happen so better things will come.

Often agreements are made, but will fall through last minute. These experiences teach you to deal with problems quickly and efficiently and stops you from becoming complacent. It gives you a reason to do more research to find an alternative, and almost always there will be a better alternative. Thanks to the former mishaps!

Don't dwell on the emotions you are feeling as a consequence of the problems you are facing, instead, just keep working on finding those solutions.

30 YOU HAVE A PLAYLIST OF MOTIVATIONAL SONGS

You are prepared!

Making playlists of motivational songs or video playlists of talks and speeches is a game changer. When you've been given disastrous news, get those playlists up to inspire and encourage you.

31 REFLECT ON YOURSELF AND YOUR BUSINESS EVERY DAY

Reflection is key.

Having the ability to evaluate yourself and your brand is absolutely vital. Whether things are going well, or not so well, reflect on how tasks were achieved or not achieved, how problems were handled and how to improve for next time. By reflecting on yourself at the end of every day, you will make a habit of improving yourself every day.

Of course, there will be days where you did an incredible job, in which case you have earned a pat on the back.

32 YOU ARE DELIRIOUS

When every cell in your body is willing for it to work, you won't want to see the negative sides of your business.

We all wish that our visions pan out smoothly, but sometimes the market is not ready for you, or your competitors have an advantage and your survival is at stake. It is difficult to be realistic, but sometimes the hardest decision is the right one.

33 YOU WILL FAIL MANY TIMES

Failure is part of the game and the many times you fall down, it will be just as hard to get back up.

Things will not go smoothly, but through the ups and downs, you will gain strength and resilience.

You won't always win the pitches for investments, you won't get the best price for your supplies, you won't have the best and most efficient product in the market. That is all ok.

You will take so much out of these pitfalls, you will learn and grow, streamline and improve. Each time you feel disappointed or disheartened, know that you took the risk, you took the opportunity placed in front of you, you had faith or even if you didn't, you still pulled through. You took this challenge on. You will question your own ability and whether it is worth getting up and trying again. Each time you fail, you will learn invaluable lessons.

You can learn from observing others' failures, but you will not fully experience it, not enough to know exactly how you should tweak your strategy to succeed - there's dignity in failure, so embrace it.

34 NO ONE WILL SEE THE 99 LUDICROUS EXPERIMENTS BEHIND THAT ONE SUCCESS

All of the sketches, drafts, deleted words and prototypes stay in the office. They will not see the light of day.

The hard work you put in doesn't go unnoticed - that one success was born out of the refinements and iterations of those explorations.

35 PEOPLE WON'T TAKE YOU SERIOUSLY

There will be people who won't take you or your idea seriously. There will be truckloads of people who don't understand your idea. All beginnings are hard - especially when your idea is in your head, you can envision it but no one else can. Keep believing. Remember why you had the idea to begin with, why you are trying to make this idea into a reality, and why you care about making it work.

I spent a lot of time approaching countless related organisations about my idea at the conception stage, to ask for support or opinions in hopes of receiving positive feedback and enthusiasm about my vision. Instead, I hit a brick wall. I was rejected right at the doorstep of many organisations after I explained what I wanted to do and who I wanted to speak to. Later, I realised the problem. I looked young, I was inexperienced and all I had was an idea, nobody was going to take me seriously. Not just organisations, but people I met, I sincerely told them what I wanted to do, my vision and my passion, but more often than not, the listener would show a look of disinterest. Others just nodded unenthusiastically and found an excuse to dismiss themselves.

It wasn't just my age and lack of experience that had people smirking at my idea when I enthusiastically shared my passion. My market is niche. When those who are not my target market heard of my idea, they said it was bizarre. They said no one wants my product, that I wouldn't go far. They didn't believe in any of my value propositions. Without support, advice and enthusiasm, I didn't know where to start and how to make my vision a reality.

If you are sure about what it is that you want to create, start researching. Do all the research you can on your competitors, the market, the demand and keep conjuring a picture, constantly adding details so you can make it clear that the market is ready for your product or service, they will demand it, and people will pay for it. If you can do this and confidently say yes to all three, then keep your head down.

There will always be people who don't take you seriously and don't believe in you, even the people you need the most at the most crucial moments, but all you need is to believe in yourself.

36 YOU ARE COURAGEOUS

There are many people around you who doubt you. You're a young adult and you look like you just don't have your shit together. That may be the case, but if you're serious, pluck up the courage and you can bring anything you want into this world and prove yourself. Even if people didn't take you seriously to begin with, they will now think more carefully about you and your product.

Your hard work reflects on your personality. You have to be strong, resilient, driven and responsible.

Taking that first step takes a dash of fearlessness.

37 SPEAK TO EVERYONE

Speak to more people about your idea. The chances are, other people would be able to give you great input. You may be afraid of a couple of things. Others may copy your idea. Well, there are probably another hundred who has had the same idea already. Also, this is your idea. You must have an advantage over others - networks, knowledge or passion which makes you perfect to execute it.

Secondly, you're afraid. You're afraid that once it becomes public, there's no going back. It will be upsetting when others ask how it went, and you would have to reveal that it failed, or you gave up.

Neither of those problems should be considered. It is incredibly useful to bounce your ideas off others. Imagine you shared your idea with someone who could help you overcome the biggest obstacle and your hugest worry about your start-up. You could meet journalists waiting for someone like you to cover an article about. Speaking openly about your idea will test it and receiving feedback will allow you to see a realistic picture of the market.

For those who have never heard of your idea, one day they will hear about it again, and at that point, they will remember you.

38 YOU WILL BE INSPIRED BY EVERYTHING

When you've found your purpose and your mind is clear about what you want to do and what you want to create, everything you come across will inspire you and motivate you.

Songs will give you strength, talks will teach you wise lessons. You listen to other people's stories and you will feel moved. Admire the beauty of everything around you, breathe it in and realise what a beautiful world it is, and how much strength you have to build your vision.

You have the capabilities to make it happen because there are so many people out there who have been through it too. And they've made it.

39 AT TIMES YOU NEED ONE BIG THING TO LOOK FORWARD TO

Cultivate leisure time.

As an entrepreneur, you have the power to choose when you work, where you work and how you work. Utilise that power to declutter your mind. Practice self-care. There have been numerous studies by neuroscientists who have shown that the best ideas come to you when your brain is relaxed.

When I found times were hard and I had a rough few weeks scheduled ahead, I booked a short trip away, it keeps you willing yourself to complete those mundane tasks, get them out of the way so you can take that well-deserved break. Even if it's something small, make some plans a month or two ahead, so you can keep looking forward to the light at the end of the tunnel!

You need a break, you're only human.

40 YOU CAN WEAR YOUR PYJAMAS WHILST YOU WORK

Being able to wear your pyjamas to work should become a global standard.

Thankfully, being your own boss means you can dress how you want. When working from home, you don't need to feel uncomfortable in a suit or high heels. Although any time you're out of the house you better be dressed in a presentable manner, you never know who you will meet and you want to ensure no one has a bad impression of you or your brand.

Say goodbye to those comfy sweatpants, the university hoodie you used to live in, they won't be seen in public. Also, those trainers are only reserved for when you're at the gym - if and when you make it to the gym.

41 IT IS EASY TO GO OFF TRACK

Whilst being able to schedule your day and wear your pyjamas are one of the biggest perks of being your own boss, it can make you become complacent. It is easy to fall into the trap of waking up, feeling groggy and granting yourself a day off. Of course, it is great to take a break from work from time to time, but recovering from one day off is as hard as it sounds.

Entrepreneurs need to be highly disciplined to get themselves back into a routine. This tests not only our self-control, but also how passionate we are about our projects. Most days we do jump out of bed in the morning thinking about the tasks of the day and are eager to finish up breakfast to start working on it.

Some days (especially when it is bright and sunny outside), we have to resist the temptation to do what our hearts desire.

42 TIDYING THE HOUSE BECOMES THERAPEUTIC

No longer do you complain about cleaning the house.

Hoovering and tidying up is so therapeutic, it takes away the stress and dull feelings of being caged in the house.

For the first time in your life, you will see your mother's impressed expression by your initiative to clean the house.

43 NO ONE IS DOING ANYTHING YOU ARE DOING

Most of us don't like to stick out like a sore thumb.

When everyone around you is talking about the same thing - going to university, getting a job, you become frightened to talk about what you want to do. You have no one to share your thoughts with. Not only because you're scared of other people's reactions, but because they won't understand.

Walking in the opposite direction to all of your friends takes a lot of courage. Be prepared that they will talk about you behind your back, they will make fun of you for 'dreaming too big', they will look down on you for not being 'realistic'.

Remember, without taking a new path, you won't discover a better place.

44 SOMEONE AT SOME POINT WILL ASK YOU 'WHY CAN'T YOU GET A PROPER JOB?'

Quite often this would come from your family. There may be friends who think this but may not always voice it. On the other hand, your family will be brutally honest and ask you to get your head straight. "What do you think you're doing carving your own path?" "Get a proper job with a proper salary please." Even if you show signs of seriousness, you're urged to have a backup plan, to find a full time job and work on this 'project' in your spare time.

Now, imagine having to juggle all of that. This is the perk of being young. You have so much time to experiment, you have the choice to not get yourself stuck in a full time job before realising that you didn't want that. Before you become complacent and scared to lose everything when quitting the day job to work on your real passion. You have a choice.

So, 'why can't you get a proper job?' Well, entrepreneurs know inside of them exactly what they don't want to do. This will push you towards paths you want to work towards. In retrospect, I think I always knew that I wanted to carve my own path. I've always loved freedom. I could create what I wanted to and loved to have full control over my work. Understanding yourself, realising what you like and don't like will help you make the leap of faith and show your family or peers how serious you are about your vision. Don't let other people's standards be put against you. People are like flowers, they blossom at different times and stages of life. You don't have to be ordinary. Do what makes you most comfortable and get a job you love, otherwise, make a job you love.

45 YOU LOVE YOUR JOB

Even through the stress of uncertainty and confusion, you love every bit of it.

You love the challenges; you love seeing people's reactions to your idea.

You love your customers, every one of them.

You love the late night emails and you love watching your brand grow.

You love entering competitions for funding, whether you win or not, you love that feeling of being pushed out of your comfort zone, and persevering through these new, yet daunting experiences.

You love to meet people who don't understand - you smile at them because you know one day, they will.

46 WHEN SOMEONE ASKS WHAT YOU DO, AND YOU DON'T KNOW IF THEY WANT THE FULL ANSWER OR THEY ARE ASKING OUT OF POLITENESS

The short answer is, I'm the Founder and CEO at _____.

The long answer - I have a start-up which I've been slaving my days away keeping it alive and actually, I haven't eaten or slept in four days, I had to write a business plan in three and pitch for funding on the fourth. Now I'm at this networking event, because I am looking for someone who can do my financials for me, since I have no clue what I've written in my business plan.

Behind the glamorous title, is a not so glamorous story.

47 YOU AND YOUR BRAND WILL KEEP EVOLVING

You're still in search of who you are, what you like, and still discovering new things. Likewise, your young brand starts off as a blank slate and you're responsible for granting it a voice and personality. You want the best for your brand and you want it to be perfect the first time round, but both life and entrepreneurship is about experimenting.

You are most likely not going to get it right the first time.

Along the way, you will change or discover something new. This is normal and very exciting. Through the process of entrepreneurship, your thoughts and perspectives will evolve at a rapid rate. It's tough to be patient when it comes to experimentations and tweaking the details - you're not the best at it yet, but eventually you will be.

48 ONE DAY YOU WILL WAKE UP AND YOU WILL KNOW IT WAS ALL WORTH IT

Behind the scenes there are countless sleepless nights, bundles of stress and times when you are knocked down.

Keep your head down. Keep working on it. Wait for that one day, trust me, it's coming.

That one day you will wake up and realise how much of an impact you have made on other people's lives because of what you have been working so hard on. On that day, you will wake up and the feeling will be indescribable.

You will be so thankful for not giving up, for seeing it through, for being the strong you, on that day, you will know it was all worth it.

49 THERE ARE MORE CHALLENGES AHEAD, BUT YOU ARE READY FOR THEM

You will meet countless obstacles and situations which cause you severe stress. Everything will seem to be falling apart. There are situations out of your control, and as a young entrepreneur, dealing with situations that are out of your control is torturous! Things are delayed, miscommunications lead to problems, previous agreements fall through... These setbacks frustrate you and you will feel like giving up.

This is inevitable.

You're strong. That's why through all of this, you still keep going. Remember: if you give up now, no one would know how hard you hustled, all the hours you put in and what your vision is.

So far you've survived a plethora of struggles already, but you're just at the beginning.

You don't know what to expect in the future as more problems will surely be thrown at you, but this is where it becomes exciting. You've only seen the tip of the iceberg; even more opportunities lay ahead when you become more established. You're ready for it.

50 YOUR ATTITUDE DICTATES YOUR ACHIEVEMENTS

Not so much your capabilities and resources, rather your attitude dictates your achievements.

At such a young age, you are not going to be the most knowledgable, nor the most skilled in the industry. Starting off will be difficult with no capital and probably no funds too. Good news is that these things are not imperative.

Your attitude greatly affects your chance of success. If you have the right attitude - you're willing to work, you know the ups and downs of entrepreneurship (well, you're bound to if you've made it up to here) and you're not frightened.

If you're ready, then go for it.

51 YOU WILL MAKE AN IMPACT ON PEOPLE'S LIVES

This is why we do it. This is why we become entrepreneurs - it's never the money. Money is a byproduct. Our passion and knowing that what we love to do can change people's lives is unquantifiable. It drives us and makes us love every challenge we face. We solve those problems so we can continue to share our passion and change the world. We take those risks because we care about this problem we are solving.

After persevering through obstacle after obstacle to land myself at this spot right now, it makes me wonder, what would have happened to all the ideas I had before if I had just gritted my teeth and kept going? It is less about regretting the ideas that did not make it to bear fruit, it is rather the realisation of how much power we have when we are passionate about something. Often times we think 'what can a small human like me do? How can I have the power to even change the world?' You can. With the passion you have, you can do anything. It sounds cliché, but if you love something enough, if you care about it enough to make it happen, it will change the world. Don't let that idea keep living in your head, transfer it into a tangible reality so you can take it with you and share it with people. The world is ready and it's just waiting for you.

AUTHOR'S NOTE

Becoming an entrepreneur, the Founder and CEO of Inspire Me Korea at the age of 21, has taught me the most valuable life lessons and continues to guide me through new experiences that I would have never imagined.

Thinking back, I had no idea what I wanted to do, but I knew that I wanted to do everything. I've always been a creative person who has a wide range of interests. In school, I opted to study more subjects than my counterparts and always loved every subject I learnt. I graduated at University College London (UCL) at 21 with an Arts and Sciences degree (BASc) - the first degree in the UK that allows flexibility to choose modules from multiple departments to create an interdisciplinary course. I studied Politics, Economics, Geography, Japanese, Business and Entrepreneurship. Alongside studies, I managed two YouTube channels, self-taught to play the Ukulele, participated in charity runs, had a part time job, volunteered and went to the gym religiously. At that time, I had no idea what I wanted to do with my career. I wanted to own something. I love brands. I eventually was set on creating a brand of my own, I just had no idea what.

After graduating at UCL, I embarked on a solo trip to South Korea to study on a summer program at Inha University, Incheon. I've been interested in South Korea for over 5 years which started from Kpop music and led to Korean culture. It was the most memorable trip I've ever made. I was touched by the Korean people who were generous, kind and loving to a foreigner, I fell in love with the rapidly developing country which manages to retain their history and culture. I would visit ancient palaces and admire the beautiful architecture, learn about the history and cultural significance, yet turn around and see skyscrapers behind me. This hybrid in the city of Seoul made me realise that such a beautiful and unique place exists.

I came back to the UK in time for my graduation ceremony and I was hit with the reality that all graduates experience. I was thrown into the real world, I had to find a job and start the 9-5 or even 9-6 hustle. I wasn't ready for this.

I believe a last gift from my late grandmother - the day of her funeral (and the day before my graduation ceremony), I suddenly had an idea. I wanted to create a subscription box service for Korean culture in the UK, which includes an array of products representing different aspects to Korea's distinct and diversified culture. I desperately wanted to make my way back to South Korea, but it was not an option, so instead, I brought South Korea here. I found the best way to live in my home country yet be able to keep that connection with the fond memories I had in South Korea. All of these amazing ideas started blowing up in my mind and I still cannot believe that the boxes I send out today, are exactly how I envisioned it that day before my graduation. To this day it feels surreal that this is my job, and being able to know what I love, do what I love, and share it with people I care about makes me eternally grateful.

An 'entrepreneur' is an incredible title, but it comes with endless responsibilities. Being an inexperienced, first-time entrepreneur and having next to zero guidance as to how to start and what to do at the beginning stages, I was met with many hardships alone. Being the sole founder is burdensome. There is a lot of pressure in this role, especially because I care so deeply about my idea having experienced the problem in learning about and accessing Korean culture myself. The greed to see my brand grow, to prove myself to those who doubted me, to make my family proud, and to show that the decision to dive into entrepreneurship straight after graduation was right for me has guided me through a tough battle.

My advice to anyone who is considering entrepreneurship is that you should never get into it for the wrong reasons. For the glory or fame. You should have an idea that you strongly believe in, an idea that you have fallen in love with and care deeply enough to keep working on it for years ahead. You want to make this idea a tangible reality and you have a burning desire to make it work. That is why you become an entrepreneur. It doesn't work the other way round. Falling in love with the idea of becoming an entrepreneur, then thinking of ideas that will make you one is unsustainable and won't keep you working hard enough in the long run. Don't waste your youth and energy working on a business you don't care enough about.

Being young is great. You have huge aspirations; you have big dreams. You're naive and you don't know what obstacles you will face just yet. You will dive into it and then realise the multitude of hurdles and challenges, but you will keep going. If I had known all of the obstacles I would have had to face before building this company, I don't think I would have started. But you have relentless drive, time, fire in you and you're naive. That is what makes a young entrepreneur so powerful.

Printed in Great Britain
by Amazon